NATIONAL GEOGRAPHIC KIDS

Animals

READY TO MEET ANIMALS FROM AROUND THE WORLD?

Here's how it works!

On the FIND IT! pages, search the image for the creatures shown at the bottom of the page. The number next to each animal's name tells you how many are hidden in the scene!

Then, on the EXPLORE IT! pages, you'll learn all about the animals you just found.

NATIONAL GEOGRAPHIC
Washington, D.C.

The Amazon
RAINFOREST

The Amazon rainforest is the largest tropical rainforest in the world. It is found in nine different countries in South America. It is filled with all kinds of trees, plants, and wildlife.

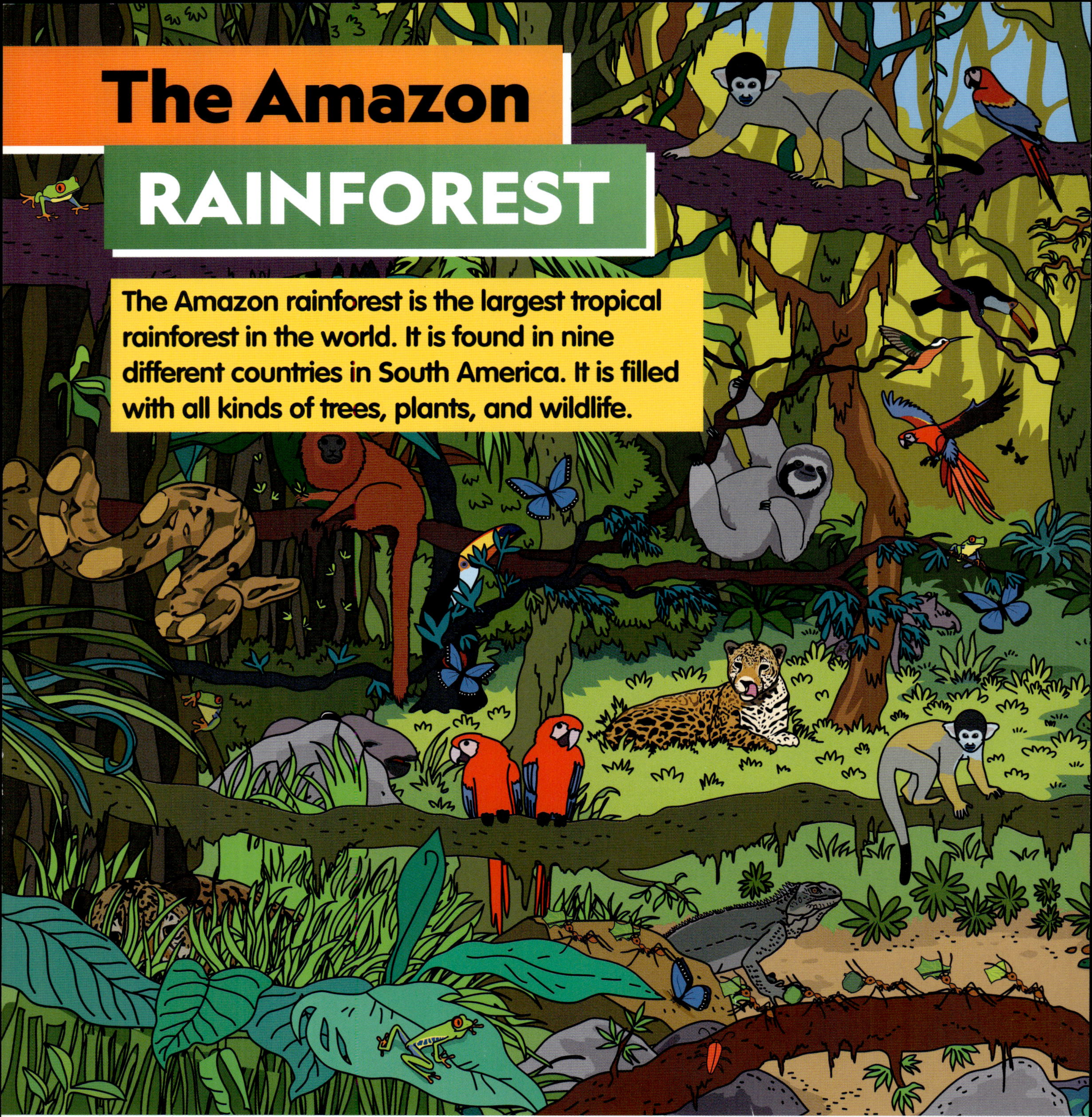

1 Green anaconda

2 Tapirs

3 Sloths

4 Jaguars

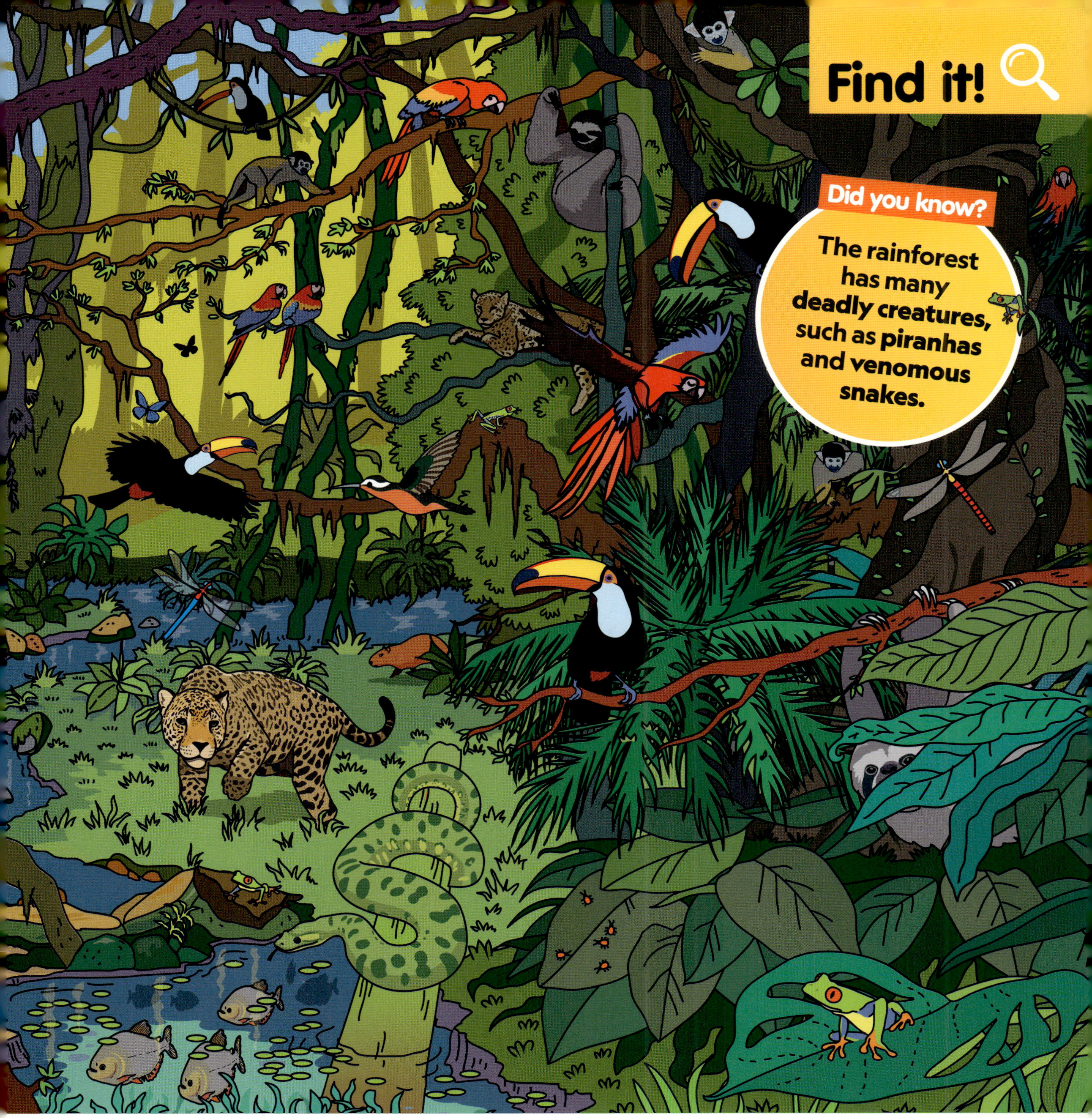

Did you know?

The rainforest has many deadly creatures, such as piranhas and venomous snakes.

5 Monkeys

6 Toucans

7 Leafcutter ants

8 Tree frogs

RED-EYED TREE FROG

Red-eyed tree frogs are famous creatures of the rainforest. They sleep during the day, underneath leaves. If they are disturbed, the frogs flash their huge red eyes and reveal their brightly colored feet and sides. This surprises predators, giving the tree frog time to get away.

Would you prefer to sleep at night, or during the day like a tree frog?

LEAFCUTTER ANTS march with chunks of leaves in their jaws. These pieces are carried back to the nest and fed to a fungus, which the ants' larvae then eat. The ants and fungus can't live without each other.

MACAW

Macaws have brightly colored feathers. They have large, powerful beaks that are great for cracking nuts and seeds. Their dry tongues have a bone inside that is used for tapping into fruits.

TOUCAN

A toucan's large, colorful bill can grow to around six inches (15 cm) in length. It is made of keratin—the same material that your fingernails are made from.

SQUIRREL MONKEY

To clean themselves, squirrel monkeys pee on their hands and then rub it over other parts of their bodies!

JAGUAR

Jaguars are the third largest big cat, after tigers and lions. Jaguars look a bit like leopards but their spot patterns are a little different—jaguar spots often have a dot in the middle.

Can you think of any other spotted animals?

GREEN IGUANAS are fast reptiles. They have powerful jaws, razor-sharp teeth, and pointed tails. If caught by a predator, an iguana can detach its tail and grow another!

SLOTH

Sloths are the world's slowest mammals. Their slow movement and the hot rainforest air cause algae to grow on their furry coat. The greenish color is useful for camouflage.

Sloths like to hang on branches. What other animals can you think of that swing on trees?

TAPIR

Tapirs look like pigs with short trunks. However, they are actually more closely related to horses and rhinoceroses. Tapirs love water and often take a dip to cool off.

GREEN ANACONDA

Green anacondas are the world's heaviest snakes—they can grow to be as long as a pickup truck. They reach their huge size by eating wild pigs, birds, and even jaguars!

The Wild
ARCTIC

The Arctic is as far north as you can go! It is one of the coldest places on the planet. Even though it's chilly, there are plenty of animals that call it home!

1 Narwhal

2 Orcas

3 Walruses

4 Polar bears

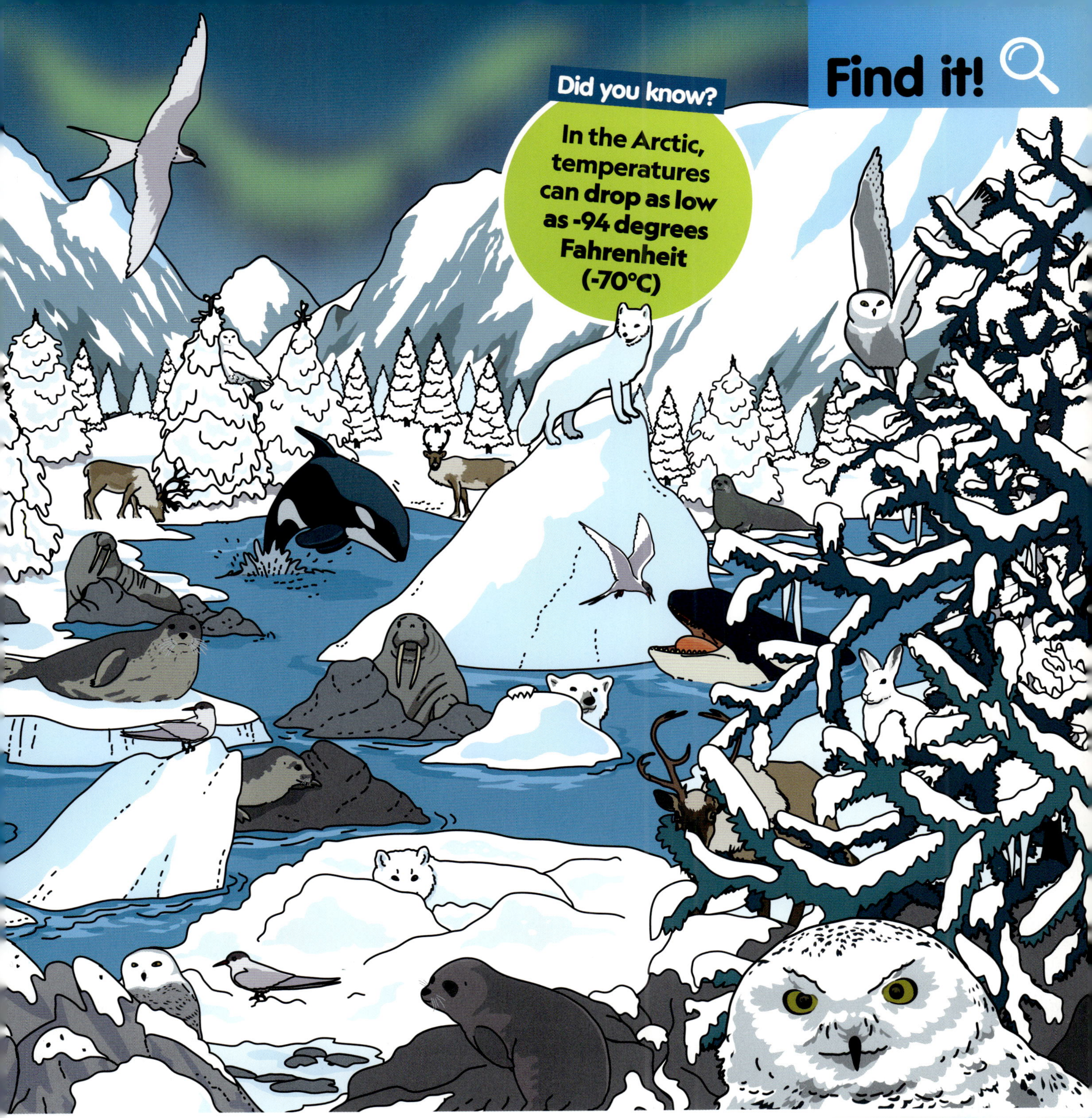

Did you know?

In the Arctic, temperatures can drop as low as -94 degrees Fahrenheit (-70°C)

5 Arctic foxes

6 Reindeer

7 Seals

8 Snowy owls

REINDEER

Reindeer are also known as caribou. Unlike most types of deer, both male and female reindeer grow large antlers. They have specially designed noses that heat up the icy cold air before they breathe it in.

Next time you are outside in the cold, take a very deep breath. Can you see why reindeer need self-heating nostrils?!

Can you think of more animals that like to eat fish?

PUFFINS are seabirds that nest on cliff faces. They dive into the water to catch fish to eat. They are known for their colorful beaks, which often carry up to 12 fish at once.

10

SNOWY OWL

Snowy owls have very thick layers of feathers. They also look like they have fluffy slippers. This is thanks to the extra feathers around their legs and feet that keep them warm.

BEARDED SEAL

Bearded seals are the largest type of seal in the Arctic—they weigh around the same as a grand piano! Their long whiskers look like a beard, earning them their name.

ARCTIC FOX

Arctic foxes have brown coats in the summer and white coats in the winter. This gives them great camouflage whatever the season.

POLAR BEAR

Polar bears are the largest carnivorous (meat-eating) land mammals on the planet. Their fur appears white, which helps keep them camouflaged in the snow and ice. Their skin is black, which soaks in the sun's rays and helps them stay warm.

NARWHALS look like unicorns of the sea thanks to the single horn on the front of their heads. But these "horns" are actually more like teeth and are very sensitive!

Would you rather be a unicorn or a narwhal?

WALRUS

Walruses are massive! They can be as long and as heavy as a car! Walruses have tusks that they use to pull themselves out of the water and to fight other walruses.

ORCA

Orcas are enormous—they are almost the same length as a bus! They are also very intelligent mammals. They work in packs and have been known to make waves to knock their prey into the sea to hunt them.

Orcas have their own language. Can you make up your own language using sounds?

European
WOODLAND

Ancient woodland usually has large trees that have been growing for hundreds of years. The old trees' curling branches can make the woodlands look spooky. They are the perfect places for wildlife to hide!

1 Tawny owl

2 Pheasants

3 Badgers

4 Hedgehogs

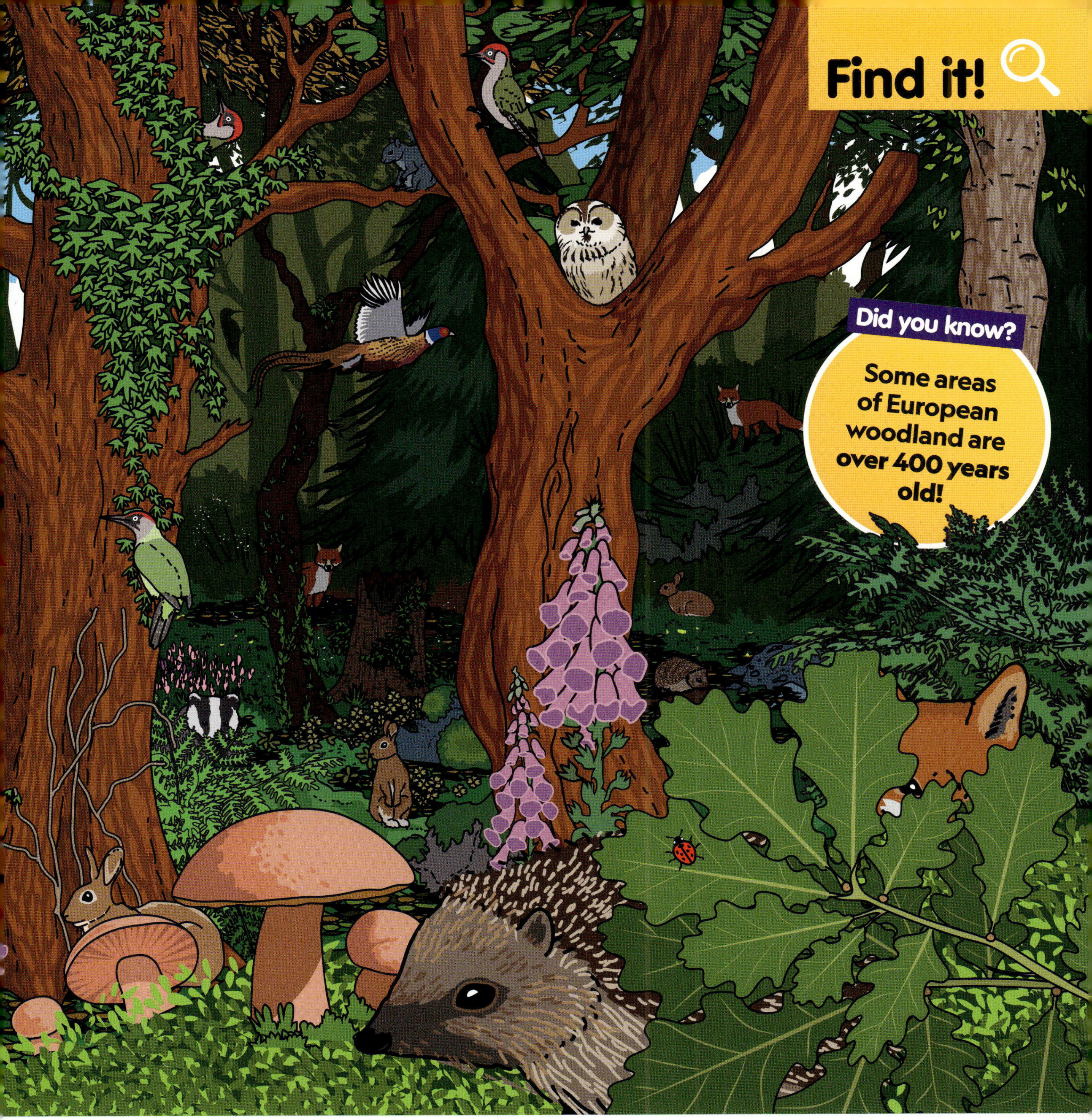

Did you know?

Some areas of European woodland are over 400 years old!

5 Squirrels

6 Foxes

7 Rabbits

8 Woodpeckers

FOX

Foxes are mammals that look like a cross between a cat and a dog. They are fast and active animals. Foxes are good hunters, too. They like to hunt rabbits, rodents, and birds but also eat berries.

GRAY SQUIRREL

Gray squirrels are playful creatures with bushy tails. They live in trees. They protect their nests by barking and wiggling their tails.

WOODPECKER

Woodpeckers are brightly colored birds. Some of them make a fast pecking sound by tapping on tree trunks.

Woodpeckers have very long tongues. Is your tongue long enough to touch your nose?

RABBIT

Rabbits, known for their long ears, live underground in connected burrows called warrens. When they are happy, they jump in the air, twisting their bodies and kicking their feet. This move is called a binky!

RED SQUIRRELS are much smaller than gray squirrels. They have tufts of fur on their ears and white rings around their eyes.

Next time you hear a bird singing, try to copy its call (and see if it responds to you).

TAWNY OWL

Like most owls, tawny owls are nocturnal. This means that they sleep during the day and are awake at night.

Can you curl into a ball like a hedgehog? See how small you can make yourself.

HEDGEHOGS are spikey little creatures that rustle through the undergrowth looking for juicy slugs to eat. A hedgehog can have between 5,000 and 7,000 spikes on its back depending on its size.

BADGER

Badgers are mammals that like to eat whatever they can find. They live in large burrows called setts. Badgers keep their homes very clean—they make sure they go to the bathroom outside.

PHEASANT

Pheasants are medium-size birds. Male pheasants (right) are very brightly colored. The females are much less flashy.

ROE DEER

Roe deer have a light brown coat. They have big black eyes and noses. The males have small antlers with three points. Deer are very athletic and can jump as high as five feet (1.5 m)—that's right over your head!

The SAHARA

Located in Africa, the Sahara is one of the largest deserts in the world! It is also one of the world's hottest places. Temperatures here have been known to reach over 122 degrees Fahrenheit (50°C).

1 Camel

2 Fennec foxes

3 Barbary sheep

4 Cape hares

Find it! 🔍

Did you know?

The Sahara is almost as big as the U.S.A.!

 **5** Gazelles

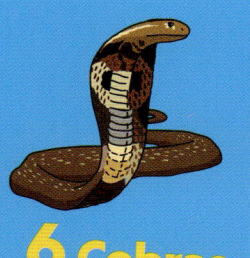 **6** Cobras

 **7** Scorpions

 **8** Jerboas

21

JERBOA

Jerboas look like mice on stilts! They come out at night and can move very fast. Jerboas jump to escape predators.

COBRA

Cobras have a hood around their head, which makes them easy to recognize. There are many types of cobras that live in the Sahara, and all of them are venomous!

GAZELLE

Gazelles look a bit like deer, but they have curved, ringed horns instead of antlers.

SCORPION

Scorpions are closely related to spiders. They have large stinging tails that curl up and over their bodies. They also have large pincers, like crabs.

23

CAMEL

Camels are large desert animals that look like llamas with huge humps on their backs. Their humps are used to store fat. The fat gives camels energy for their treks across the hot desert when there isn't much food or water.

What's your favorite desert animal and why?

FENNEC FOX

Fennec foxes are some of the smallest foxes around, with some of the biggest ears! Their ears aren't just big to help them hear; they help them to cool down, too.

BARBARY SHEEP

Barbary sheep are great at jumping. They can leap 6.6 feet (2 m) high, which is higher than the height of most adult humans.

CAPE HARE

Cape hares have large eyes, good eyesight, and long ears. These hares sometimes eat their own droppings!

25

The Rocky
MOUNTAINS

The Rocky Mountains run through Canada and the U.S.A. The mountains have lots of different types of weather, which means many different kinds of animals live here.

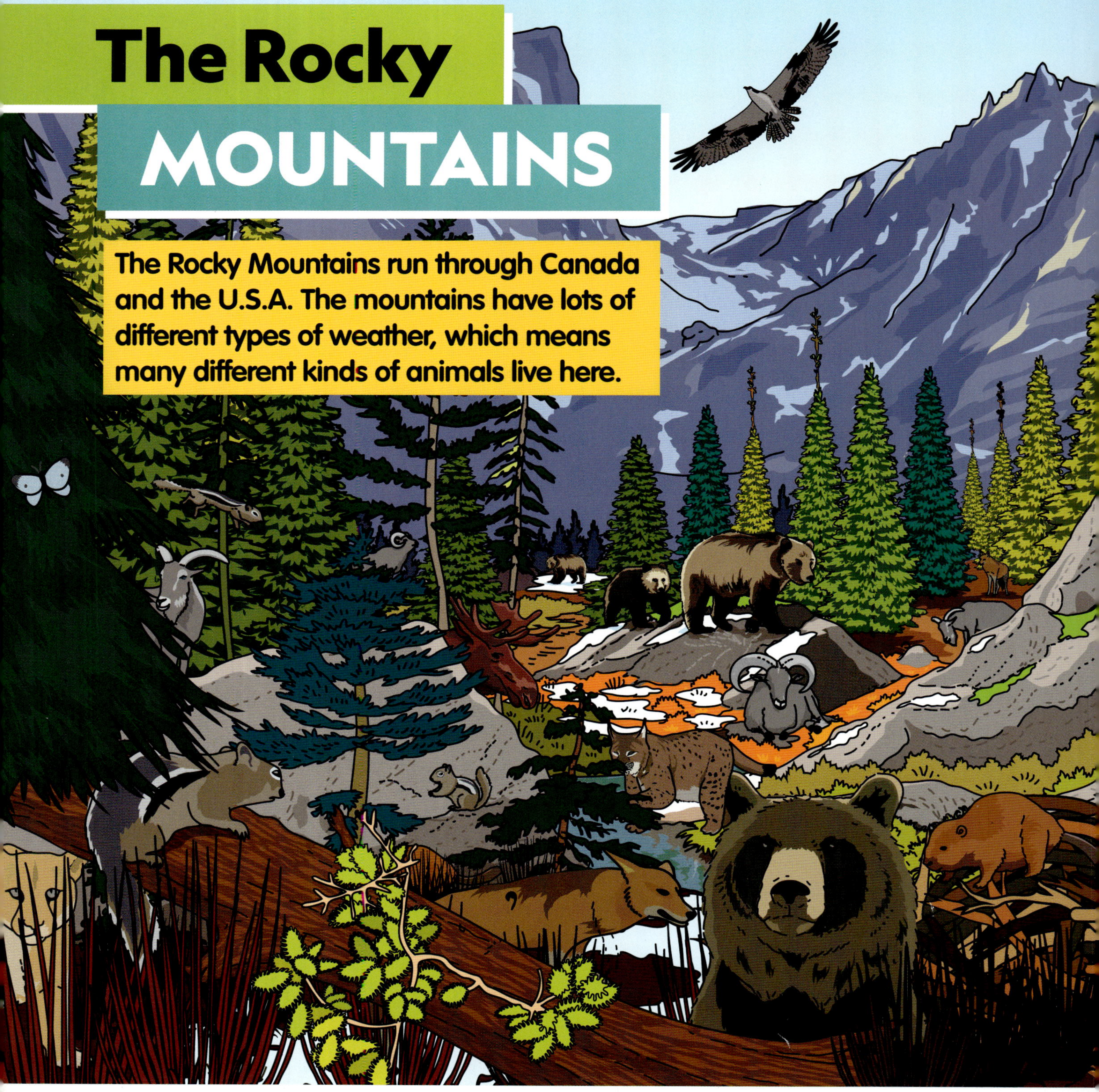

1 Lynx

2 Mountain lions

3 Coyotes

4 Moose

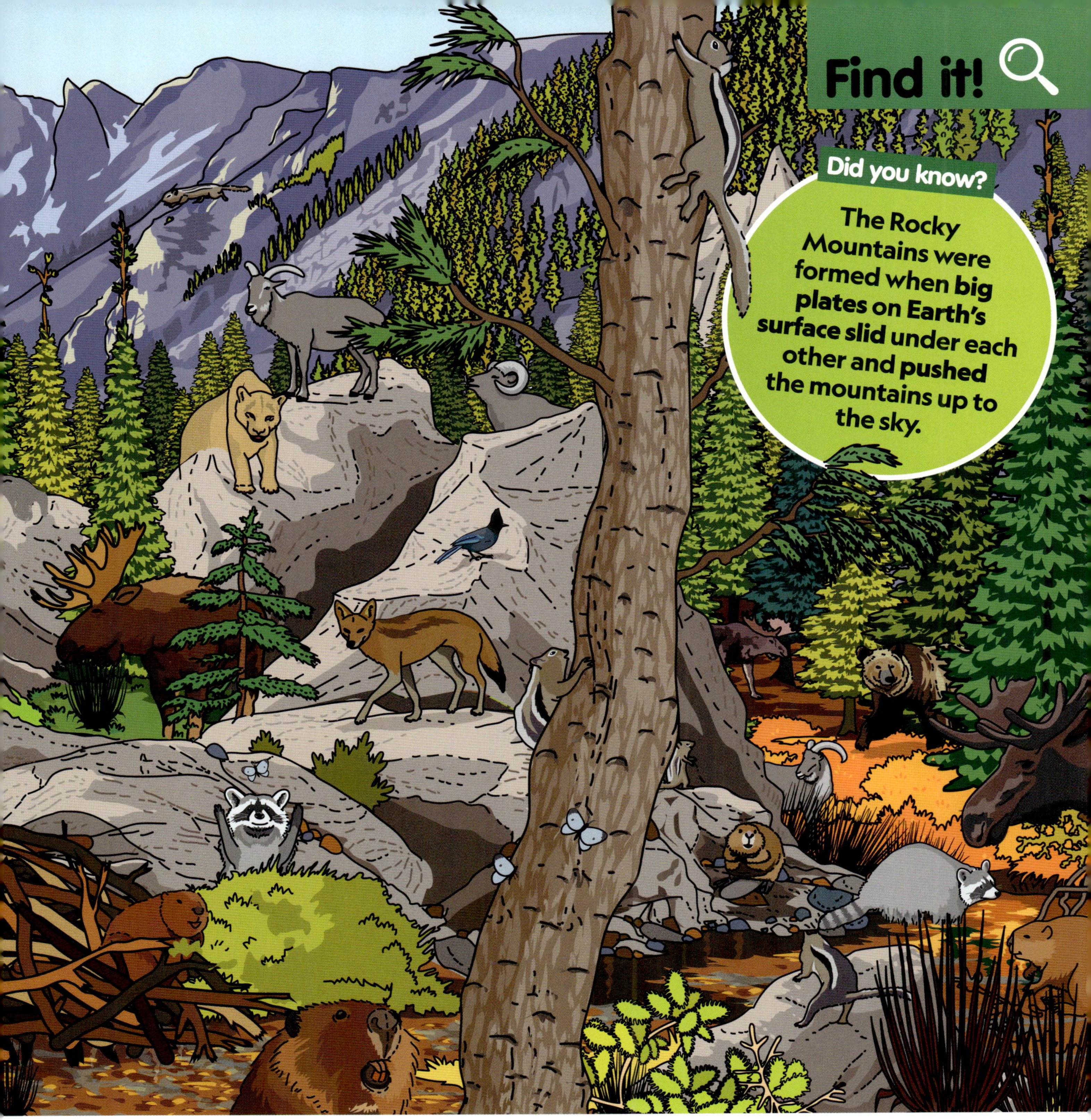

The Rocky Mountains were formed when big plates on Earth's surface slid under each other and pushed the mountains up to the sky.

5 Grizzly bears

6 Beavers

7 Bighorn sheep

8 Chipmunks

BEAVER

Beavers are furry mammals. They have big teeth for chomping through trees and bark. They have flat tails that help them swim and can also be slapped against the water to signal danger!

COYOTE

Coyotes are like small wolves. They like to hunt at night, and they have great eyesight and a good sense of smell. They have been known to chase prey for miles before eventually hunting it down.

Can you howl like a coyote? Give it a try!

BIGHORN SHEEP

Bighorn sheep live on the slopes of the Rocky Mountains. They have huge curled horns. Bighorn sheep in the Rockies grow much bigger than bighorn sheep that live in other places.

GRIZZLY BEAR

Grizzly bears are very large meat-eating mammals. The big hump on a grizzly's back is a muscle the bear uses for digging.

Can you puff up your cheeks like a chipmunk?

CHIPMUNK

Chipmunks look like striped squirrels with very stretchy cheeks! They hibernate in the winter but wake up every now and again for a nutty snack.

BLACK BEAR

Black bears come in many colors, including black, red, and blond. When they hibernate during the winter, they do not eat, drink, or go to the bathroom.

MOUNTAIN LION

Mountain lions are also called cougars. They are big cats that can move quickly and leap long distances!

LYNX

Lynx are medium-size cats with fluffy tips on the end of their ears. They have short tails, and their back legs are longer than their front legs. This helps them pounce!

MOOSE

Moose are the biggest species of deer in the world. Every moose has a pouch of skin called a bell that hangs from its neck. Male moose have enormous antlers.

Would you rather have horns or antlers?

RACCOON

Raccoons have some of the most skillful hands in the animal kingdom! Their name means "animal that scratches with its hands," and they are known for gathering food with their humanlike fingers.

The Australian BUSH

The Australian bush is a name given to wooded natural areas of Australia. Hardly any people live in the Australian bush, but plenty of animals do!

 **1 Platypus**

 **2 Wombats**

 **3 Emus**

 **4 Echidnas**

5 Dingoes

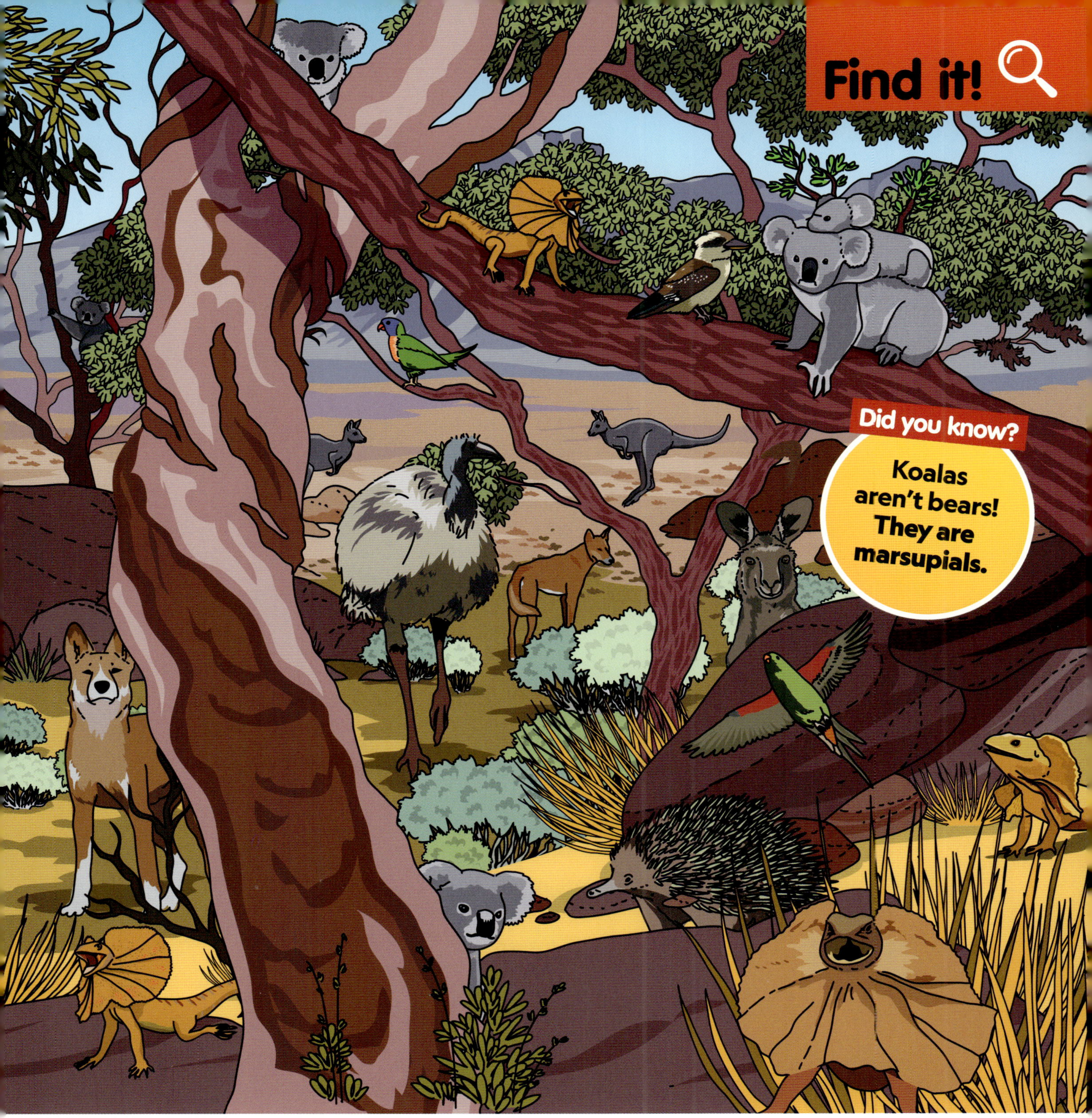

6 Kangaroos

7 Koalas

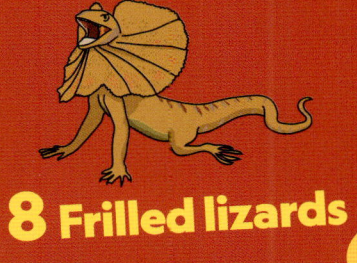

8 Frilled lizards

KANGAROO

Kangaroos are the largest marsupials in the world. A marsupial carries its babies in a pouch!

If you had your own pouch, what would you keep in it and why?

REDBACK SPIDERS are closely related to black widow spiders and are very venomous. They usually eat insects and other spiders but have been known to eat larger animals such as lizards.

If you could have a bright color on your back, what color would you choose?

FRILLED LIZARD

Frilled lizards have big frills around their necks. The frills are used to scare away predators. The lizards also hiss and run, if they need to!

DINGO

Dingoes are wild dogs with large wedge-shaped heads. They howl and chatter, but rarely bark.

PLATYPUS

Platypuses are strange-looking animals. The body of a platypus is similar to an otter's. It has a bill and webbed feet like a duck and a tail like a beaver's.

KOALA

Koalas are small gray marsupials that spend most of their time sleeping. They sleep for more than 18 hours a day! When they aren't sleeping, they are eating lots of eucalyptus leaves.

KOOKABURRAS are the largest member of the kingfisher family. They have large heads and beaks. They are also known for their call, which sounds like they are giggling!

How long can you laugh? Try it with a friend or your family—you might make each other laugh, too!

ECHIDNA

Echidnas look like a cross between a hedgehog and an anteater. They are amazing because they are one of only two mammals in the world that lay eggs! The other is the platypus.

Which Australian bush animal is your favorite and why?

EMU

Emus are the second tallest bird in the world, after the ostrich. They have soft, fluffy feathers and long, powerful legs. Emus can't fly, but they can run very fast!

WOMBAT

Wombats are great at digging thanks to their claws and barrel-shaped bodies. The pouch of the female wombat faces backward so that soil doesn't get in it when she digs.

The Serengeti
PLAIN

The Serengeti Plain is in Tanzania, Africa. It contains many habitats, such as forests, swamps, and grasslands. These places are home to lots of different types of animals.

1 Hippopotamus

2 Rhinoceroses

3 Leopards

4 Elephants

Find it!

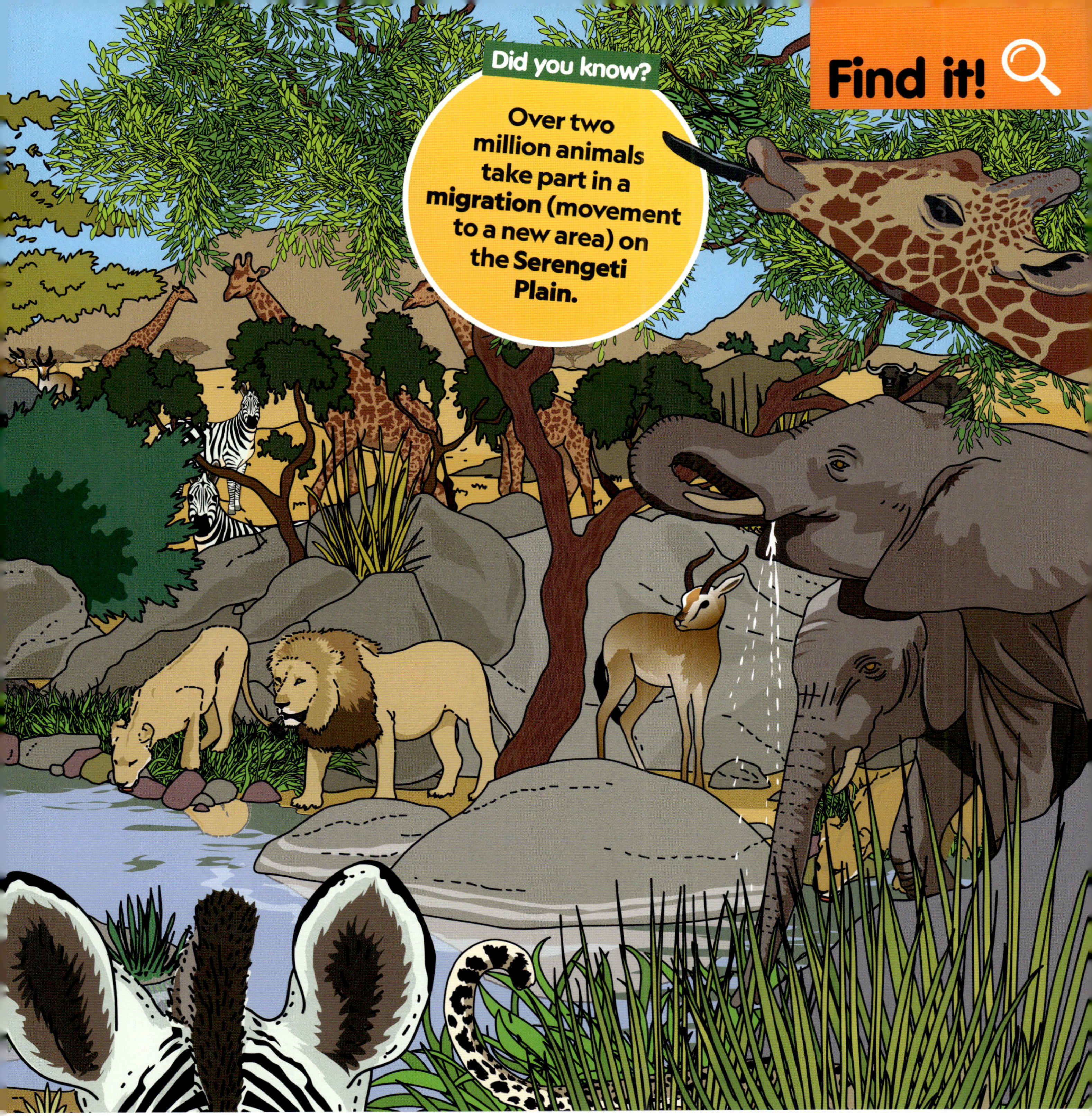

Did you know?

Over two million animals take part in a migration (movement to a new area) on the Serengeti Plain.

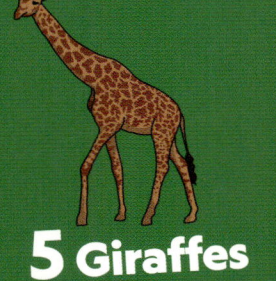

5 Giraffes **6** Buffalo **7** Lions **8** Zebras

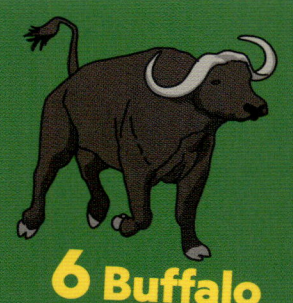

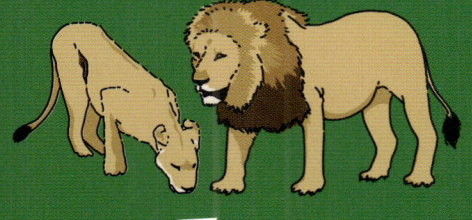

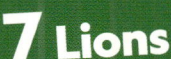

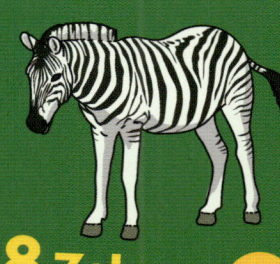

ZEBRA

Zebras are known for their striped pattern. Each zebra's pattern is unique. This means no two zebras are the same.

Which Serengeti animal would you most like to see in the wild?

LION

Lions are known as the kings of the animal world. They have powerful bodies, and males have bushy manes. Lions live in groups called prides.

BUFFALO

Buffalo are amazingly strong. They live in herds that can be made up of more than a thousand buffalo!

Which animal feature would you like to have? The power of a lion? The height of a giraffe? Or the strength of a buffalo?

GIRAFFE

Giraffes are the tallest animals in the world! With their extremely long necks, they can stand well over 16 feet (5 m)! That's as high as three adult humans standing on top of each other!

What do you like most about elephants?

ELEPHANT

Elephants are the biggest land animals in the world. They have excellent memories—they know and remember each member of their herd. Their big brains are capable of recognizing more than 30 different elephants!

CHEETAHS are the fastest land animals and the fastest runners in the world. They also have great balance. This is how their heads stay so steady when they run at speeds of over 56 miles an hour (90 km/h)!

LEOPARD

Leopards are powerful, clever big cats. They often pull their prey onto branches of trees so they can eat in peace!

If you were an animal, would you rather have spots or stripes?

RHINOCEROS

Rhinoceroses are very strong and very fast. They have sharp horns on their noses and have a keen sense of smell. They are the second largest land animal.

HIPPOPOTAMUS

Hippopotamuses are dangerous animals. They are strong and aggressive, and have very big teeth. Their bite is so powerful that it can snap a canoe in half.

SOLUTIONS

The Amazon Rainforest

The Wild Arctic

European Woodland

The Sahara

The Rocky Mountains

The Australian Bush

The Serengeti Plain

Where in the world can you find the places in this book? Check out the map below.

The Wild Arctic

European Woodland

Europe

North America

Asia

The Rocky Mountains

The Sahara

Africa

The Amazon Rainforest

South America

Oceania

The Serengeti Plain

The Australian Bush

Antarctica

Trade Paperback ISBN: 978-1-4263-7578-1
Reinforced Library Binding ISBN: 978-1-4263-7583-5

The contents of this publication are believed correct at the time of printing. Nevertheless the publisher can accept no responsibility for errors or omissions, changes in the detail given, or for any expense or loss thereby caused.

Since 1888, the National Geographic Society has funded more than 14,000 research, conservation, education, and storytelling projects around the world. National Geographic Partners distributes a portion of the funds it receives from your purchase to National Geographic Society to support programs including the conservation of animals and their habitats. To learn more, visit natgeo.com/info.

Illustrations by Steve Evans

Photo Credits

NPL: Nature Picture Library; SS: Shutterstock

Cover (toucan), Scanrail1/SS; (tree frog), Worldswildlifewonders/SS; (squirrel monkey), Ludmila Ruzickova/SS; 1, Brian Lasenby/SS; 4, Worldswildlifewonders/SS; 5 (UP), David Havel/SS; 5 (CTR), Scanrail1/SS; 5 (LO), Ludmila Ruzickova/SS; 6, Jo Reason/SS; 7 (UP), Enrico Pescantini/SS; 7, (CTR) Ben Queenborough/SS; 7 (LO), Andrew J. Clark/SS; 10, Dmitry Chulov/SS; 11 (UP), Jim Cumming/SS; 11 (CTR), Danita Delimont on Offset/SS; 11 (LO), NaturesMomentsuk/SS; 12, Chase Dekker/SS; 13 (UP), Ondrej Prosicky/SS; 13 (LO), Christian Musat/SS; 16 (UP), AB Photographie/SS; 16 (LO), Douglas Jennifer/SS; 17 (UP), aaltair/SS; 17 (LO), Nigel Dowsett/SS; 18, Ondrej Prosicky/SS; 19 (UP), Edward Hasting-Evans/SS; 19 (CTR), Marcin Perkowski/SS; 19 (LO), WildMedia/SS; 22 (UP), reptiles4all/SS; 22 (LO), tb-photography/SS; 23 (UP), Nabil Refaat/SS; 23 (LO), Protasov AN/SS; 24, Shengyong Li/SS; 25 (UP), hagit berkovich/SS; 25 (CTR), Alexander Sviridov/SS; 25 (LO), Katy Foster/SS; 28 (UP), Danita Delimont/SS; 28 (CTR), Warren Metcalf/SS; 28 (LO), Chris Curtis/SS; 29 (UP), Islandwave/SS; 29 (LO), Brian Lasenby/SS; 30 (UP), Troutnut/SS; 30 (CTR), Gabriel Rojo/NPL; 30 (LO), Oriol Alamany/NPL; 31 (UP), Michael Liggett/SS; 31 (LO), Papa Bravo/SS; 34, Damian Lugowski/SS; 35 (UP), Ken Griffiths/SS; 35 (CTR), John Carnemolla/SS; 35 (LO), Lukas_Vejrik/SS; 36, Yatra4289/SS; 37 (UP), Jukka Jantunen/SS; 37 (CTR), Ken Griffiths/SS; 37 (LO), Sonijya/SS; 40 (UP), Mari Swanepoel/SS; 40 (LO), Maggy Meyer/SS; 41 (UP), 2630ben/SS; 41 (LO), Planet Earth/SS; 42, Kletr/SS; 43 (UP), Michael_Edwards/SS; 43 (CTR), MM.Wildlifephotos/SS; 43 (LO), PhotocechCZ/SS

Printed in China
23/LPC/1